Both God and Money

PERSONAL FINANCE

ACCORDING TO GOD'S WORD

© Steve Puersten, 2014

Contact Steve directly:
steve@puerstenbookkeeping.com
(647) 885 9321

CONTENTS

1 You Cannot Serve
2 Budgeting 101
3 Debt
4 Saving and Investment
5 Giving
6 Live Simply…and Generously

YOU CANNOT SERVE...

*No servant can serve two masters:
for either he will hate the one, and love the other;
or else he will hold to the one, and despise the other.
You cannot serve both God and money*

-Luke 16:13

Money - a relatively short word: five letters, two syllables, two vowels, three consonants. But, packed into that seemingly innocent little word is a lot of meaning. It doesn't matter whether we:

- $ have a lot or a little,
- $ have more than we need or are resentful because we don't have our share,
- $ are constantly looking for ways to squander what we do have, or
- $ dream of wealth beyond our means

Money is a word that stirs emotions and imaginations like few others. It can provide vast power and influence or it can bring utter and total ruin. It can polarize people's thoughts and feelings. And our thoughts and feelings surrounding money can even provoke violence.

Our world attaches much significance to money. Many sayings like:

- $ 'Money makes the world go round',
- $ 'Money is the root of all evil',
- $ 'A penny saved is a penny earned' and
- $ 'A fool and his money are soon parted'

....

have become staples in our culture and reflect just a few of the ways in which we think about and, sometimes even, worship money.

© STEVE PUERSTEN, 2014

The [Merriam-Webster Dictionary](#) defines money as:

> *"something (such as coins or bills) used as a way to pay for goods and services and to pay people for their work."*

That makes money a tool, created to serve man much the same way as a hammer or a shovel. *But more and more we are seeing money becoming the master and man the servant.*

What do I mean by that? How could this have come to be? I will address these questions as we move through the book, but I will say here this scenario has evolved due to a perfect storm of factors, including our advertising culture and availability of credit – to name just a few.

As a mere medium of exchange, money, itself, is neither good nor evil. Yet people use it, not only to fund great projects to advance our knowledge or to resolve hunger or poverty issues around the world, but also to wage war and create vast fortunes, in spite of the ruin it brings to others. *How can all of this come from a mere tool?*

The problem is not due to money itself. Rather, the problem comes from how we think about and react to money. We get caught up in a cycle, in the same way we get caught up abusing alcohol or drugs, or worshipping the rich and the famous: it can cause us to lose our perspective and even bring us to ruin. Similarly, the love of money clouds our judgment and also brings about our destruction.

© STEVE PUERSTEN, 2014

Money in the Bible

The importance of money is addressed in the Bible. The word 'money' is used in the Bible more than 800 times and you can find more than 2350 verses concerning money and financial principles. There are verses concerning budgeting, investing, debt, tithing and many more. The sheer depth and breadth of these topics throughout the Bible show not only does God consider the issue very important, but also He is very concerned about our financial well-being and *empowerment through managing our money*.

We all desire to be comfortable financially and since God created us, it makes sense He desires that for us too. In fact, God says:

> *For I know the plans I have for you, declares the LORD,*
> *plans to prosper you and not to harm you,*
> *plans to give you hope and a future.*
> ~ Jeremiah 29:11

Since God is concerned about our prosperity, it makes sense to find out what His thoughts are so we can benefit from His guidance.

First of all, God makes it very clear EVERYTHING belongs to Him:

This world and everything in it belongs to God.

> *The earth is the Lord's, and everything in it,*
> *the world and all who live in it*
> –Psalm 24:1

Consequently, if everything belongs to God, then it stands to reason that actually we do not own anything. Rather, we are entrusted by God to take care of His creation for Him (Wow! Not

© STEVE PUERSTEN, 2014

only does that change how we look at our money, but also, it gives us a fresh resolve to do a better job of handling what has been given to us.):

> *What is man that you are mindful of him,*
> *the son of man that you care for him?*
> *You made him a little lower than the heavenly beings*
> *and crowned him with glory and honour.*
> *You made him ruler over the works of your hands;*
> *you put everything under his feet*
>
> *-Psalm 8:4-6*

Nowhere in the Bible is this idea that man is entrusted to care for God's Creation better illustrated than in the "Parable of the Talents", where God makes it clear He holds us accountable for what we do with "our" money:

> *For it will be like a man going on a journey, who called his servants and entrusted to them his property. To one he gave five talents, to another two, to another one, to each according to his ability. Then he went away.*
>
> *He who had received the five talents went at once and traded with them, and he made five talents more. So also he who had the two talents made two talents more. But he who had received the one talent went and dug in the ground and hid his master's money.*
>
> *Now after a long time the master of those servants came and settled accounts with them. And he who had received the five talents came forward, bringing five talents more, saying, 'Master, you delivered to me five talents; here I have made five talents more.' His master said to him, 'Well done, good and faithful servant. You have been faithful over a little; I will set you over much. Enter into the joy of your master.'*

And he also who had the two talents came forward, saying, 'Master, you delivered to me two talents; here I have made two talents more.' His master said to him, 'Well done, good and faithful servant. You have been faithful over a little; I will set you over much. Enter into the joy of your master.'

He also who had received the one talent came forward, saying, 'Master, I knew you to be a hard man, reaping where you did not sow, and gathering where you scattered no seed, so I was afraid, and I went and hid your talent in the ground. Here you have what is yours.' But his master answered him, 'You wicked and slothful servant! You knew that I reap where I have not sown and gather where I scattered no seed? Then you ought to have invested my money with the bankers, and at my coming I should have received what was my own with interest. So take the talent from him and give it to him who has the ten talents.

For to everyone who has will more be given, and he will have an abundance. But from the one who has not, even what he has will be taken away. And cast the worthless servant into the outer darkness. In that place there will be weeping and gnashing of teeth

–Matthew 25:14-30

When we look at our lives today, the Parable of the Talents can help us appreciate how we have been entrusted to multiply God's money for the greatest good of humanity and the earth itself. The first two servants illustrate how to consider different vehicles to invest the money God has given us, such as – as an example - more volatile stocks versus more conservative GIC's or bonds.

The amount of money the Master gave to each of the servants in this Parable was *according to his ability*. The Master understood each of his servants had different skills and would make his investing decisions according to his skillset and sensibilities surrounding money. In other words, each of those two servants chose according to his circumstances and comfort level with risk, in addition to their ability.

Of course, the critical lesson from this Parable lies with the choice the third servant made. He let fear take over, which ruled his outlook and final decision. Even though the third servant had less money to work with and, likely, he would have made even more conservative choices than the other two servants, he didn't share the trust the Master had in him. Instead of investing the talent to earn over time, he hid it to guarantee he could return it to his Master.

How did you react when the Master took away that one talent? Did you think he was overly harsh?

When you think about it, if you only keep the cash you have on hand, never investing it and allowing it to grow, you will lose even that amount. Life hands us situations, sometimes at a moment's notice, such as emergencies, sudden changes in career or lifestyle choices, tuition for your children and more. When those situations crop up, if we have no reserves then we have to dip into the money we need for our everyday life. Then, we have lost even our base amount. In these cases, we cannot take care of even our needs and those of our family, much less help others in our community or the world.

God expects us to enhance what He has entrusted to us.

Jesus on Money

Jesus says much on the topic of money. He talks about giving to the poor, not cheating others and being satisfied with what you have. He speaks most scornfully, however, about the love of money:

> *For the love of money is the root of all evil:*
> *which while some coveted after, they have erred from the faith,*
> *and pierced themselves through with many sorrows*
>
> *-1 Timothy 6:10*

After the rich young ruler walked away upset, because he was told to sell all of his worldly wealth and give the proceeds to the poor, Jesus says:

> *How hard it is for the rich to enter the kingdom of God!*
> *Indeed, it is easier for a camel to go through the eye of a needle*
> *than for a rich man to enter the kingdom of God*
>
> *-Luke 18:24-25*

This presents an awkward image to say the least, and it illustrates very well if you are too attached to your money, it can be very hard to be attached to God at the same time.

The Money Trap

Money can become a trap very easily, a never-ending cycle from which it is hard to escape. It is easy to think if only you had a bigger house, or a newer car, you would be happy and not need anything else. Or you may feel if you can live as well as your neighbours, your life will be complete. You might think 'I work hard, I deserve to have a break' and consequently spend whatever it takes to quench your sense of entitlement.

Yet all of that is an illusion, a mirage that disappears the moment you get to it. Once you buy the bigger house, the newer car, or, finally, acquire your neighbour's lifestyle, you set out to get an even bigger house, newer car, or a pool like the neighbour just got... At this new level, you fall back into the cycle all over again. When you make choices, based on that sense of entitlement, you end up only putting yourself into debt, and desperately trying to scramble out of the hole you dug for yourself. In fact, God speaks of precisely this in the Bible:

> *Whoever loves money never has money enough;*
> *whoever loves wealth is never satisfied with his income.*
> *This too is meaningless*
>
> *-Ecclesiastes 5:10*

Sometimes, we convince ourselves if only we had enough money, we wouldn't worry about what will happen to us. Just like the example above, when we chased increasing amounts of money and what it buys to boost our self worth, we hope money will protect us from the unknown. The trouble is, no amount of money can remove worry because our "reasoning" is not based on the truth of God's peace. By pursuing money in those ways, just like the mirage in the desert, our ever-elusive goal of happiness and content evaporate.

I am reminded of a story of a man who had his debt consolidated using the equity on his home. He proceeded to run up his credit cards again, and consolidated all over again. At the time I was told this story, the man wanted to consolidate a third time but he was told the equity train had run out and he would not be able to do so.

It is human nature to want more than one has. While it's true people have always been this way, it is also true the financial picture for the average person in the developed world has changed. The birth of the middle class and the consumer culture, the rise of aggressive advertising and the easy availability of credit all have conspired to put pressures on people that didn't exist before.

© STEVE PUERSTEN, 2014

How do we deal with this changed environment? Since God knows and loves His people, He has provided guidance for all of these issues in the Bible. Let's look at what God has to say...

Budgets

*For which of you, intending to build a tower, does not sit down first
and count the cost, whether he may have enough to finish it;
perhaps, after he has laid the foundation and is not able to finish,
all those seeing begin to mock him, saying,
this man began to build and was not able to finish*

-Luke 14:28-30

Let me tell you a story of two couples: Although the first couple brought over $100,000 a year into their household from both their well-paying jobs, they had neither bought a home, nor had they saved enough for a deposit to buy one. Additionally, they owed considerable debt, which they couldn't get a handle on. Additionally, most of their debt was consumer debt, or bad debt, which is more costly... but I'll explain this more in the chapter on debt.

The second couple never filed income taxes for more than $40,000 in any given year. Despite that, they lived in a modest home, paid a mortgage and still found a little money to contribute to an RRSP.

What is the difference between these two couples? Actually, there are several, but one of the more significant differences between the two is the second couple budgets while the first does not. They track their income and expenses month by month and use the resultant information to plan their future expenses.

[Merriam Webster](#) Dictionary defines a budget as: *"a plan used to decide the amount of money that can be spent and how it will be spent"*.

The prospect of budgeting strikes most people as dull and inconvenient, or even unnecessary, but it is essential to getting a handle on your money. In fact, the foundation of responsible financial management is the budget. Just like the builder who does not count cost before building, the person who doesn't do a rudimentary plan (a budget) can't expect to succeed financially.

Our current society encourages people to buy whatever they desire, whenever they desire it, with no concern for the future. Often, to achieve this, people rely on credit.

The RBC Economics Research site reports the debt-to-income ratio hit 150.5% in the first quarter of 2013. That means average Canadians are spending routinely more than 1 ½ times their disposable income. When you spend more than you have on a regular basis, your debt load continues to climb… and you stay in debt forever.

The Benefits

Not only is there an ever-present pressure to keep up appearances, but also, as I will show you, life and financial management are more complicated now. First of all, we have more places these days for you to direct money in your budget. Also, today's calculations for mortgages and credit card interest are more complex. These considerations make it even more important to keep a careful eye on your finances.

Your budget is a practical and necessary tool to keep control of your personal finances. By first tracking your expenses, then using the resultant data to set target amounts for all your budget lines, suddenly, it becomes possible to have financial control.

© STEVE PUERSTEN, 2014

With a little tweaking and practice working with the numbers, and some discipline to stick to the numbers you set, the exercise of preparing a budget and the satisfaction of achieving your goals will definitely pay off.

Disposable Income

What is disposable income?

Google defines it as: *"income remaining after deduction of taxes and other mandatory charges, available to be spent or saved as one wishes"*.

A Gallup poll in June 2013 reported only one third of Americans choose to use a budget to track their personal finances. This means the majority of people do not know where their money is spent, or how MUCH is available to them.

And what are these "other mandatory charges"?

If you are like most people, you pay a mortgage or rent every month. Also, you have regular car, insurance and utility payments. These expenses are unavoidable and you may have them withdrawn automatically from your bank account. The amount of each of these expenses does not vary from month to month; they are called 'fixed' expenses.

'But the rest is mine, right?' you may ask. Actually, no. After the fixed expenses are paid, there are more costs, such as: phone, grocery, automobile gas, and home and car maintenance expenses. The outlay for these are unavoidable too. Since the amount for these costs varies monthly, they are called 'variable' expenses.

Finally, after fixed and variable costs, and after money has been set aside for retirement and some for savings, whatever is left is yours to spend as you wish.

'Hold it!' you say, 'That's not much left over. While that's probably true, it's also reality. You cannot avoid the truth. You cannot spend more than you make. That is Budget 101.

BUDGETING 101

The first concept of budgeting is: what goes out needs to be less than what comes in. If you're not budgeting, how can you know you're spending less than you earn? The truth is, without a basic budget, you can't.

The most basic way to budget is to figure in your head what is left after you subtract what you've spent from what you've made. Considering how complex life is and how many areas you need to direct your money, figuring rough calculations as you go is not a very practical option.

The Bank Statement

Your monthly bank statement gives you a great snapshot of your financial situation. Think about it – your monthly statement is a itemizes transaction by transaction everything that goes in and out of your bank account. That may seem deadly obvious, yet, shockingly, many people never bother to look at this.

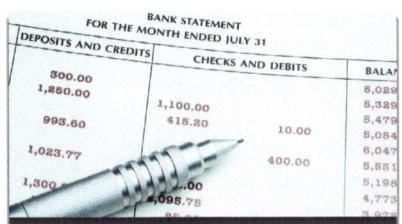

© STEVE PUERSTEN, 2014

In fact, in 2012, Barclays did a study in the UK of how many people (out of 9 million) delayed or completely avoided opening their monthly bank statements. They coined this phenomenon as 'Chronic Banxiety'. Although their study shows a national variance within the UK (25% London; 37% Wales; 44% Scotland; 68% N. Ireland), within those results, 60% of those suffering from 'banxiety' delayed opening their bank statements for the following reasons:

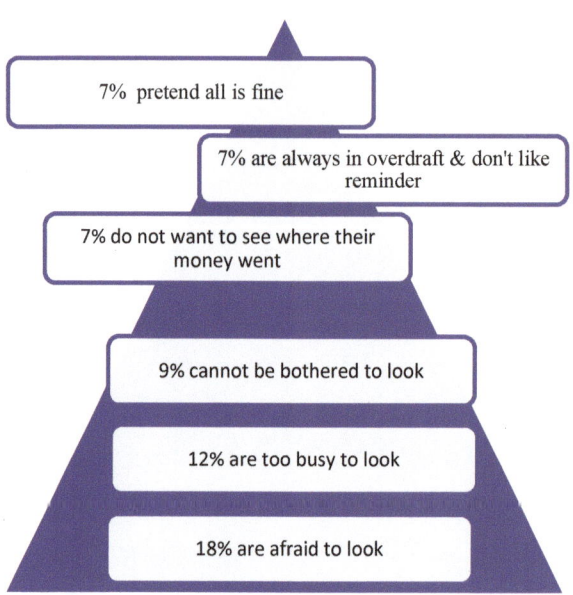

Additionally, Barclays found 13% of all people polled are less likely now to open their bank statements than 5 years ago (when the economy was better). Most eye-opening of all, Barclays found the largest demographic of those least likely to open their monthly bank statements is young adults. In fact, 55% of 18-24 year olds put off opening their bank statements compared to the national average of those who delay dental appointments (48%).

Don't be one of those people! Commit to opening your bank statements right away. It's one of the most basic, yet important steps you can take to understand and manage your budget. In fact, most banks offer online tools to help you analyze your monthly finances.

The Ledger Book

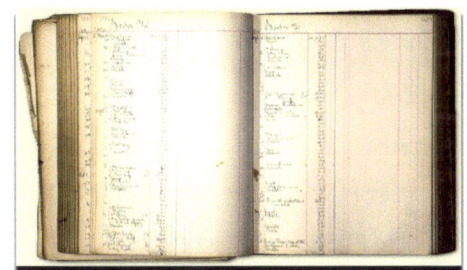

When I was a boy, my father gave me a little, black book. Inside, there were columns and rows and at the top of each page he had labelled the columns for: Date, Item, Received, Paid and Balance.

With this basic ledger book, I was expected to track all of my income, expenses and to account for all the money I was entrusted to my keeping. If the amount of money I had didn't match the amount at the bottom of the balance column, questions were asked! I didn't much care for the book at the time, but it gave me a basic understanding of the accounting process.

Once upon a time, business owners tracked all their transactions in a ledger book. This was very much like my childhood ledger. It provided columns for the type of transaction, for the amounts received, the amounts paid, and the resultant balance.

Typical entries might look like this:

Date	Item	Received	Paid	Balance
10/5	Pay	3000.00		3000.00
10/6	Groceries		150.00	2850.00

If this is how you choose to record your finances, you can buy a basic ledger book in most business stationery stores.

© Steve Puersten, 2014

The Computer Spreadsheet

In our current technological age, you may require a higher degree of sophistication. It is fairly easy to set up an Excel spreadsheet to track all your financial information. With rows set up for income, fixed and variable expenses, you have all you need to monitor your daily, monthly, or even yearly finances. You can set up columns to compare actual numbers to what you budgeted. Also, you can set up progressive pages for each month and include a summary spreadsheet at the end.

Your basic spreadsheet could look a little like this:

Income	**Actual**	**Budget**
Salary		
Total		

Fixed Expense

Mortgage		
Car payment		
Insurance		
Total		

Variable Expense

Utilities		
Groceries		
Auto fuel and repairs		
Telephone		
Total		

Income minus expenses

© STEVE PUERSTEN, 2014

Of course, this list is by no means exhaustive. You can add to it, as needed, but I like to keep things simple. I recommend using as few line items as possible - at least at first.

To run monthly totals, simply input the amounts from your monthly receipts (What? You didn't keep them?) into each category in the cell provided. The spreadsheet will give you the current balance at any given moment.

The spreadsheet I use **(and which I will offer a copy to you, dear reader, at the end)** has a cell where the opening bank account total appears and the closing balance is automatically calculated from the spreadsheet totals. Then, these totals are compared with the monthly bank statement (Yes, you need to look at that too).

If you have never done a budget before, I recommend you go through this exercise for a few months to look through the monthly sheets and to observe the patterns. This will give you a basis of how much to put into each category of your budget. You can change the numbers anytime, as needed.

The simplest outline of how to budget is to assign target amounts to spend, in each area that you spend money monthly. This is the basis of your financial plan.

Begin with your income. Since you know what you make on a monthly basis (You do know that now, don't you?), this is easy to input. Use pay stubs and/or your bank statements. Remember, if you receive any government payments or interest on investments, this is income as well, and it needs to be reflected in your spreadsheet.

© STEVE PUERSTEN, 2014

Obviously, there is not much you can do about your fixed expenses, so this is easy to calculate, as well. As a general rule of thumb, your total housing expenses should be in the vicinity of thirty percent. If your housing costs much more, it cuts into money you need in other categories. You will see quickly how knowing this figure comes into play when considering where to live and what you can afford. Your other fixed expenses relate mainly to your previously negotiated payments for automobiles, insurance and internet.

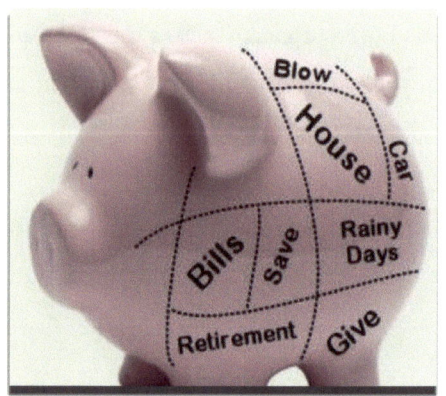

To calculate totals for your variable expenses, add up your receipts for transportation (include gas, public transit, car repairs, etc), food (groceries AND eating out), utilities (gas, water, electricity), telephone (home AND cell), cable, and input them into the spreadsheet.

Also, take into account everything you spent on clothing, entertainment, savings, charitable giving, and including all expenses (and interest) put on your credit cards.

Housing should be no more than 30% of your income. In other budget areas: transportation should be about 20%; food should be 15%; savings about 10%; and tithing should be 10%. In case you weren't counting, that is 85% of your total income... AFTER TAXES!

That leaves you with 15% of your income to do with as you please.

© STEVE PUERSTEN, 2014

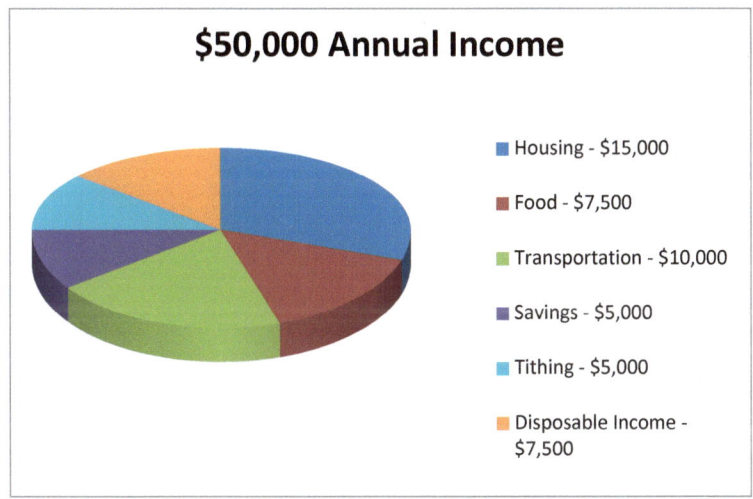

As a practical example, if you make $50,000 per year, you would have $6,375 a year (or $531 a month) of disposable income, IF YOUR BUDGET FOLLOWS THESE GUIDELINES. Now consider that many people:

- $ don't make $50,000 a year
- $ spend considerably more on housing to live well
- $ spend considerably more in many other areas to keep up with the Jones' (clothing, cars, jewellery, vacations)
- $ eat out regularly because it's convenient
- $ spend in a particular area that's important to them (i.e. private school)
- $ have debt repayments which was not included here

You can see how quickly your income is eaten up by the common habits of our modern life. This makes it all the more important to keep a close eye on every area you spend money, so financial ruin does not sneak up on you.

On the first day of every week, each of you should set aside a sum of money in keeping with his income, saving it up, so that when I come no collections will have to be made

-1 Corinthians 16:2

© STEVE PUERSTEN, 2014

DEBT

> *The rich rules over the poor,*
> *and the borrower becomes the lender's slave*
>
> *-Proverbs 22:7*

And now comes the racy part of the book. When you picked up a book about Christian money management, I don't imagine you expected to find four letter words being tossed about. Still, the word 'debt' has carried a bad connotation even from the time of the Exodus of the Israelites from Egypt:

> *If a man borrows anything from his neighbour,*
> *and it is injured or dies while its owner is not with it,*
> *he shall make full restitution*
>
> *-Exodus 22:14*

From the beginning of the nation of Israel, God has promised a blessing to those who follow him:

> *For the Lord your God will bless you as he has promised you,*
> *and you will lend to many nations, but you will not borrow;*
> *and you will rule over many nations, but they will not rule over you*
>
> *-Deuteronomy 15:6*

In our current culture, debt is still a four letter word. The view of debt has always been everyone should live within his means and if he needs to borrow, repayment in full is expected as quickly as possible.

As we learned in the chapter on budgeting, first of all there are the unavoidable expenses, such as taxes, mortgage, car payments, utilities, insurance expenses. Everything left over is disposable income which is to be used for everything else. The problem comes when a disproportionate amount of disposable income is used to purchase things for personal desires or entertainment. In these cases, people finance with credit and end up with consumer debt.

For most of human history, when anyone wished to buy something, he had to have cash. Even for purchases as large as a home, people had to save for years to have the money to complete the purchase. It wasn't until the 1930s the consumer mortgage was created. Then, in the late 1950s, the credit card was invented and a whole new world of consumer spending became available. Ever since then, lenders have enjoyed a position of great power.

Actually, in our current society, it is desirable to live with a certain amount of debt.

"What??" you say. Yes, you read that correctly.

Lenders have created a tool called the credit score. Many of your financial habits, such as paying your bills on time or requesting additional credit, are evaluated monthly. Your responsible handling of debt is translated into a score, which all lenders use to evaluate your relative risk as a borrower. When you wish to buy or finance something, your score plays a huge part in whether it's possible for you to make those purchases.

© STEVE PUERSTEN, 2014

In evaluating debt, there are better kinds of debt to incur. In essence, good debt is when you borrow for the overall benefit to your financial situation. On the other hand, bad debt is when you use credit for things which have no financial or lasting value, and are purchased for temporary gratification.

Good Debt Versus Bad Debt

Could you say more about good and bad debt?

In general, real estate, such as when you buy a home or property, is considered a good investment because the value of a home will appreciate, usually, over time. At the very least, property will never depreciate in value. Typically, it will become more valuable. Therefore, there is a benefit to the investor, which offsets the cost of the debt.

You could argue another example of good debt is when you take out a loan for post-secondary education tuition. Upgrading your skills benefits your lifestyle and increases your income over the long term. Therefore, if the debt is paid off in a timely way, the long-term gain outweighs cost of the loan debt.

Please note, however, even "good" debt can be an unbearable weight to carry. If you don't pay it off on time, interest charges increase the amount owed and add unnecessary levels of stress to your life. Let me say that again: Any debt, if not paid as quickly as possible, is a burden.

© STEVE PUERSTEN, 2014

The story in Chapter One ("You Cannot Serve") about the man who kept using equity to consolidate his debt should serve as a sobering warning about what can happen when we let our desires get the best of us. Thinking back, you may wonder why it was considered bad debt, since he used the equity in his home (real estate) to consolidate. Consolidating, in itself, is not a bad move. In his case, however, he never paid down his debt. Instead, he repeatedly used the equity on his property, to increase his financial burden until he ran dry his ability to borrow credit.

Certainly, there are many ways to incur bad debt. The notion of bad debt boils down to debt incurred to finance goods or services that are purely convenient, entertaining or do not appreciate in value. As money.cnn.com further clarifies, *"Bad debt includes debt you've taken on for things you don't need and can't afford"*.

Bad debt consists largely of credit card balances, but can also include car loans or unsecured lines of credit. For example, your new pair of shoes may feel really good to own, but its value goes to almost nothing immediately. You will never get back the amount you paid for them, let alone see them increase in value.

I mentioned car loans, and you may think a large purchase like a car is an investment. In fact, except in cases of rare or collectible automobiles, the value declines the minute you drive the car off the lot. Once again, you will never be able to reclaim the original value.

When credit cards were first invented, they were created to help people make a purchase with short term credit. Charge cards (which you pay the balance off in full each month) were the precursor to credit cards (which allow you to carry revolving credit).

Western Union came out with a charge card in 1921, followed by the Air Travel Card in 1934. By the 1940's, Diners Club and American Express were available commonly.

While charge cards were designed to be paid off, in full, monthly, credit cards became available in the 1950's, offering revolving credit. Although it's still the best strategy to pay off the full balance each month when you use a credit card, many people don't do that. Carrying revolving credit is a way of life for most people nowadays.

In fact, according to the Financial Consumer Agency of Canada (FCAC), 20% of Canadians admitted they used their credit card to pay expenses when they ran out of money during this past year. That works out to be about 4.5 million adult Canadians. In the US, CNN reported in May 2012, that 40% of low and middle income households used credit cards to pay basic living expenses, such as gas, groceries, mortgage, rent, utility and insurance bills.

It may seem like a good plan to use your credit card to buy these basic necessities, yet your living expenses are monthly expendable goods and services. If you continually "borrow from Peter to pay Paul", you are entering a downward spiral of bad consumer debt.

© STEVE PUERSTEN, 2014

The Cost

As I mentioned, no debt, good or bad, if managed correctly, is necessarily a bad thing and can even contribute to your perceived value to the banks. This will make it easier for you to access credit for other purchases.

Remember there is a cost for the use of the money whenever you enter into any borrowing agreement. For any borrowing transaction you accept, be it a mortgage, a car loan or even a credit card, you must enter into an agreement with the lender. This agreement spells out the terms of the loan, including a fee assessed by the lender. Typically, this fee is assessed as a percentage of the value of the loan and is called interest. Interest is the cost of borrowing money.

When you borrow money in the form of a mortgage or a car loan, you and the lender agree upon a fixed amount of time for the repayment of the loan as well as the rate of interest. Sometimes these things can be negotiated to the benefit of both parties.

A June 2013 moneysense.ca story lays out numerous examples when buying a house, such as arranging a higher interest rate and in return the lender allows you to make extra payments and thereby pay off your mortgage early. Another example of both parties benefitting is when you borrow money you know you can pay back quickly and easily. This is a great way to begin to build credit when you are young and just starting out or if you have are re-building your credit rating.

Looking at a credit card agreement, if you carry a balance, the debt and interest can be made to last forever. This means the cost of borrowing continues to grow as long as the debt remains unpaid.

Compound Interest

Like Michael and Jane in "Mary Poppins", many of us were taught about compound interest when we first opened a bank account. We were told, "if you invest your tuppence, wisely in the bank" that our invested money gains interest at a regular interval. Further, as the amount grows, then interest is assessed on the new amount. This means, over time, we will gain interest even on our previous interest.

As we all know, interest on the average bank account has all but disappeared. Interestingly, the banks and credit card companies have taken the basis of compound interest and used it to their advantage.

From the minute a credit card charge passes thirty days, interest is assessed on the amount owed. If the full balance is not paid then after the next thirty days, interest is assessed again. Yet it is not only assessed on the new purchase amount, but also it is assessed on the previously unpaid amount + the interest already assessed. With credit card interest charges as high as 30% (almost one third of the principle amount), it does not pay to carry a balance on your credit card.

Let's take the example of one hundred dollars charged at 10% interest:

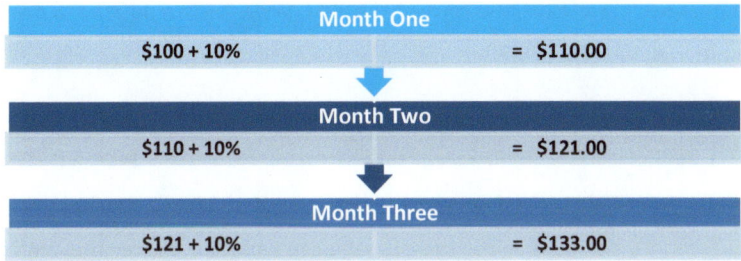

© STEVE PUERSTEN, 2014

As you can see, the interest mounts pretty quickly. By carrying the balance, the 10% charge ended up a staggering 30% over 3 months! You are paying one third the cost of your purchase to the bank for the privilege of delaying payment. Imagine that for a minute! Let me remind you, this example takes into account the effect of only one charge.

Let's look what happens when we add another one hundred dollar charge per month:

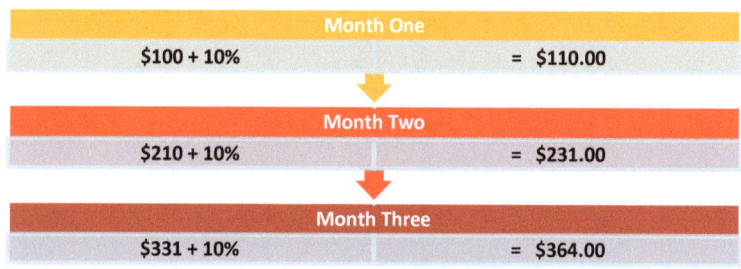

In this second example, after the first month's interest is assessed, not only is interest charged again on the purchase, but also it is charged on the previously unpaid interest. You can see how fast an unpaid balance can multiply!

There is no question we have ushered in an era of unprecedented convenience for consumers. By creating mortgages, bank loans and consumer credit cards, we can have whatever we want, when we want it.

Of course, many people use these tools just as they need to be used: to create a better life for themselves, with a reasonable return on investment for both the borrower and the lender. Unfortunately, far more people only see the convenience and their desire. They end up way over their heads, buried in a debt load, and paying vast amounts of interest on consumer debt with little or no hope of digging themselves out of the hole.

What we have is a recipe for disaster:

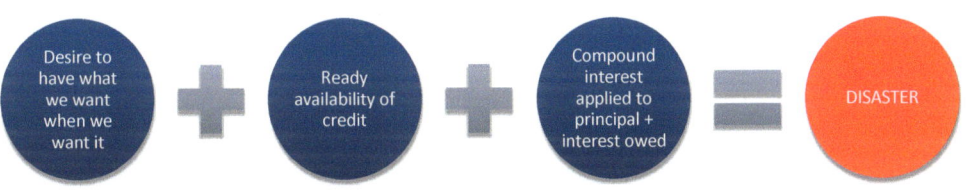

The sheer volume of people, buried under mountains of debt because they have allowed circumstances to sneak up on them, is huge. According to Statistics Canada , the number of consumer bankruptcies filed in 2013 was 69,224 and the number of consumer proposals filed was 49,454. These numbers represent 118,678 people who have allowed their financial situation to overcome them.

If more people chose to budget, these numbers would be lower. Budgeting gives you a proper grasp on your income versus your expenses. Consequently, those who don't budget, don't understand when they get paid how much of their income is actually disposable.

Clearly, it is essential to get a grasp on your financial situation, to know what your disposable income is and spend accordingly. Furthermore, since debt has a cost, called interest, it makes financial sense to negotiate shorter terms and/ or lower interest rates when taking out a mortgage or a car loan.

The largest issue comes with credit card debt. Interest rates on credit card debt are so large and with compounding of those interest rates, the danger of carrying your debt and interest rates forever is very real. It makes sense to pay off credit cards in full, to avoid carrying charges. You can do this only when you know how much you have to spend in the first place, and not exceed that amount. Then, and only then, can you get proper control of your financial situation and can never be able to say:

> The wicked borrows and does not pay back,
> but the righteous is gracious and gives
>
> –Psalm 37:21

© STEVE PUERSTEN, 2014

SAVING AND INVESTMENT

The plans of the diligent lead to profit
as surely as haste leads to poverty

-Proverbs 21:5

Life can be a very messy business with unexpected occurrences such as illness, injury, death, job loss, car breakdowns, unexpected home repairs.... The list goes on and on. Not only does each of these impact our emotional, stress-filled schedules, but also each impacts our financial schedules deeply, as well.

I'm sure you've heard the saying 'Pay yourself first'. This is a directive meant for you to put something aside for your future.

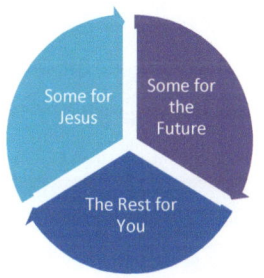

Growing up, every time we acquired a little money, I remember hearing Dad say: 'some for Jesus, some for the future, the rest for you'. He meant to impress upon us the lifelong lesson of first always giving of our firstfruits to God, and also to have something left for later.

Unfortunately, many people live as if nothing unexpected is ever going to happen and they spend all their money as if it was disposable income. When something does come up, they have nothing left, and need to dip into their credit.

On the first day of every week each of you is to put aside and save,
as he may prosper, so that no collections be made when I come

-Corinthians 16:2

© STEVE PUERSTEN, 2014

Actually, the above scripture verse refers to making collections to support other churches, but the concept is still sound. As a part of your budget (remember that?), it is good practice to put aside a part of each pay: first for tithing; then for savings; pay the bills and the rest is yours. So, 10% for Jesus, 10% for the future and the rest is for life.

When you save, begin by setting aside some funds as an emergency fund. This is money you have saved just for those moments when life brings a surprise.

If you're one of the lucky (*or prudent, from following these practices*) few who has more money than you need, you can be a hobby investor – someone who invests money in the stock market. This has made many people very rich indeed. It is very uncertain, however, and infinitely more people have lost everything by investing in stocks. If you test the waters, allocate funds to learn how to invest. The amount you invest should be excess funds – meaning you can afford to lose every penny invested.

An even sketchier practice is to buy lottery tickets regularly ([25% of Canadians play weekly](#)). I've seen lots of people in the grocery stores religiously buying fistfuls of lottery tickets. Largely, this is just wasted money as the odds of winning are so low as to be almost negligible ([1 in 28.6 million](#)). This is in the same league as the people lining up to give their money to all the casinos springing up everywhere. There are lots of stories of [people who spend](#) much of their income or have lost their very living, looking for that one big strike:

> *He who tills his land will have plenty of food,*
> *but he who follows empty pursuits will have poverty in plenty.*
> *A faithful man will abound with blessings,*
> *but he who makes haste to be rich will not go unpunished*
>
> *-Proverbs 28:19-20*

Since most of us are unlikely to hit a big strike, we are left with more conservative, more conventional (and more profitable!) options to choose.

© STEVE PUERSTEN, 2014

Once you have saved an emergency fund, it's time to save also for the future, such as your retirement and your child's education.

The simplest way to save for retirement is to open another bank account and put a set sum each month in there regularly - each pay, each month, or as often as you see fit. Remember, however, a regular bank account does not give a great return on investment. Since your savings goal is long term and you do not to need access to the money right away, it is better to look for an investment fund. There are lots out there. If you wish to protect the money from taxes while investing, then an RRSP might be right for you. Your bank manager or financial advisor can help you sort through the possibilities.

When you save for your children's education, an RESP might be the option for you. This is registered with the government. As you contribute, the government contributes on top of your amount. Imagine! Free money!

Whatever your solution, the premise is the same. You have a regular, day to day bank account and then you contribute regularly to the following: a separate account for an emergency fund; another account (or RRSP) for your retirement; and yet one more account (or RESP) for the kid's education.

Let's look at that again... There's your pay, minus the fixed expenses, minus the variable expenses, minus the emergency fund, minus the retirement fund, minus the education fund. I know, right? That's a lot of places to funnel your money into and it probably doesn't leave much afterward, does it?

And have you thought about insurance? I know. It's one more expense, but one that can lessen the impact of the unexpected. Automobile insurance is absolutely indispensable, especially when you find yourself in an accident. In most of North America, automobile insurance, at least for public liability, is mandatory. This ensures people and vehicles affected by you are taken care of within the limits of the policy. In addition, consider collision insurance. While it costs a little bit more, it ensures your vehicle and your health are protected as well.

Life insurance is another investment which will prove very wise if, heaven forbid, illness or death strikes your family. According to the [TD Insurance Risky Business Poll](), thirty one percent of Canadians do not have life insurance. When income is taken away from the family, the financial effect on your family can be devastating. The godsend of life insurance can give you freedom to manoeuvre while you get your bearings straight and your situation in order.

Several years ago, my wife and I made the decision to purchase life insurance. The agent helped us calculate how much we needed to tide us over if one of us passed away. We proceeded to pay a monthly premium toward that goal.

When my wife died four years ago, I have to admit the money provided from our life insurance policy made a huge difference as to how my daughters and I were able to move forward, at least financially, with our lives. I keep up my policy so my kids will be provided for if something happens to me.

The Benefits

What does God say about the benefits of saving for the future?

We find the thought of planning for the future really well-illustrated in the Book of Genesis. In Chapter 41, we join Joseph, who has been put in charge of all of Pharaoh's resources, after he foresaw a great famine in a dream:

> *Let Pharaoh take action to appoint overseers in charge of the land,*
> *and let him exact a fifth of the produce of the land of Egypt*
> *in the seven years of abundance. Then let them gather all the food*
> *of these good years that are coming, and store up the grain*
> *for food in the cities under Pharaoh's authority,*
> *and let them guard it. Let the food become as a reserve*
> *for the land for the seven years of famine*
> *which will occur in the land of Egypt,*
> *so that the land will not perish during the famine*
>
> *–Genesis 41:34-36*

You may feel daunted by the prospect of saving money in our current economic times. You may think investing for the future (like your retirement or your children's post-secondary education) is inconvenient. Consider the alternatives if you don't plan ahead. The thoughts of living on the street and saddling your children with crippling debt to pay their own tuition are likely inconceivable to you.

Looking again at Joseph's story, although he never foresaw how things were going to turn out for him personally, he kept going, faithfully following God's guidance. In every stage of the story, he provided value, as best he could, right where he was planted. In the end, not only was he blessed, but also he saved his family and all of Egypt.

To that same end, you can see now, I hope, how important it is to cover the basics:

- $ look at your budget,
- $ get a handle on your consumer debt and
- $ make an effort to provide for the future of you and your children.

I promise you, if you do these 3 seemingly small steps, you will be amazed at how the results will carry you.

© STEVE PUERSTEN, 2014

GIVING

> *Bring the whole tithe into the storehouse,*
> *so that there may be food in my house,*
> *and test me now in this, says the Lord of hosts,*
> *and I will open for you the windows of heaven*
> *and pour out for you a blessing until it overflows*
>
> *–Malachi 3:10*

There are few issues more contentious in the Church today than tithing. How did the model of tithing begin? Is tithing a valid Biblical belief? Does it have relevance for us today?

The Bible introduces tithing right off the bat in the book of Genesis. We join Abraham, in Chapter 14, just after he returned from defeating an army which had taken captive his nephew Lot, his family and all of his possessions. Upon his return, in which he recovered Lot and all his possessions successfully, Melchizedek, king of Salem, brought provisions to Abraham and blessed him. Abraham insisted on giving a tenth of everything to Melchizedek as a kind of payment or thanksgiving.

In Genesis 28, Jacob continued the custom after his dream at Bethel:

> *If God will be with me and will watch over me*
> *on this journey I am taking*
> *and will give food to eat and clothes to wear*
> *so that I return safely to my father's house,*
> *then the Lord will be my God and this stone*
> *that I have set up as a pillar will be God's house,*
> *and of all that you give me I will give you a tenth*
>
> *–Genesis 28:20-22*

© STEVE PUERSTEN, 2014

From then on, the concept of giving back to God is a recurring theme. Several times throughout the book of Exodus, God commanded His people to give back to Him from all He provided to them:

> *Do not hold back offerings from your granaries or your vats.*
> *You must give me the firstborn of your sons.*
> *Do the same with your cattle and your sheep*
>
> *-Exodus 22:29-30*

and

> *Celebrate the Festival of Harvest with the firstfruits*
> *of the crops you sow in your field*
>
> *-Exodus 23:16*

By the time God gave the laws to the Israelites, the notion of tithing - giving God a tenth of everything you own - was written into law:

> *A tithe of everything from the land,*
> *whether grain from the soil or fruit from the trees,*
> *belongs to the Lord; it is Holy to the Lord*
>
> *-Leviticus 27:30*

As a result, giving back to God became an Old Testament law, and it has been embraced largely by the Christian Church ever since. Today, it continues to serve as a reasonable measuring stick to guide your giving.

Now, when Jesus died on that cross in Israel all those years ago, we were released from the bonds of the Old Testament law. Instead, we were bound by a new set of rules based on the

© STEVE PUERSTEN, 2014

fact we no longer paid for our sins with animal sacrifices, and now all our wrongdoing was paid for by the sacrifice of Jesus. What does this mean for us when it comes to tithing?

While it's true tithing was an Old Covenant custom and under the New Covenant we are no longer bound by the previous law, Jesus makes it plain the spirit of the original law is still very much in force:

> Do not think that I have come to abolish the Law or the Prophets;
> I have not come to abolish them but to fulfill them.
> I tell you the truth, until heaven and earth disappear,
> not the smallest letter, not the least stroke of a pen,
> will by any means disappear until everything is accomplished
>
> -Matthew 5:17-18

In fact, not only does He make it clear we are responsible still for all our actions, including our sin, but also He turns up the heat:

> You have heard that it was said to the people long ago,
> Do not murder, and anyone who murders
> will be subject to judgement.
> But I tell you that anyone is angry with his brother
> will be subject to judgement,
> ...But anyone who says You fool
> will be in danger of the fire of hell
>
> -Luke 21-22

and

> You have heard that it was said
> Do not commit adultery.
> But I tell you that anyone who looks at a woman lustfully
> has already committed adultery with her in his heart
>
> -Luke 27-28

© STEVE PUERSTEN, 2014

With those points in mind, Jesus makes it plain what the *new standard for tithing* is:

*And he sat down opposite the treasury,
and began observing how the people were putting money into the treasury;
and many rich people were putting in large sums.
A poor widow came and put in two small copper coins.
Calling His disciples to Him, He said to them,
Truly I say to you, this poor widow put in more
than all the contributors to the treasury;
for they all put in out of their surplus,
but she, out of her poverty, put in all she owned,
all she had to live on*

-Mark 12:41-44

In other words, within the framework of the New Covenant, Jesus does not expect us to follow the Old Testament law. Rather, He expects us to exceed it. He expects us to give generously, not just from our excess, but from our firstfruits. He expects us to give out of our very living, to give until it hurts:

*Remember this:
Whoever sows sparingly will also reap sparingly,
and whoever sows generously will also reap generously.
Each should give what he has decided in his heart to give,
not reluctantly or under compulsion, for God loves a cheerful giver.
And God is able to make all grace abound to you,
so that in all things at all times, having all that you need ,
you will abound in every good work*

-2 Corinthians 9:6-8

Additionally, He expects us to give without grumbling:

*Give generously to Him and do so
without a grudging heart;
then because of this
the Lord your God will bless you
in all your work and
in everything you put your hand to*

-Deuteronomy 15:10

Furthermore, He expects us to actually give, not just in intent:

*If a brother or sister is without clothing and in need of daily food,
and one of you says to them, 'Go in peace.
Be warmed and be filled' and and yet you do not give them
what is necessary for their body, what use is that?*

-James 2:15-16

Not only has God expected you to give back to Him from the very beginning, but also He expects you to support yourself, your family and your community generously on an ongoing basis.

While you should be giving at least a tenth of your income to your church, as those funds pay a number of financial obligations including your Pastor's salary and the church's various ministry and outreach programs, you may consider contributing to other programs such as your local food bank, or one of many local or  overseas mission programs available. Remember, God will hold you accountable one day for how you managed what was entrusted to you.

© STEVE PUERSTEN, 2014

While this book aims to focus on ways to be responsible with your financial resources, you need to consider the idea of giving generously of your time to God as well. You may find it worthwhile to serve at your church, or for a local charity. Or perhaps, you can donate food or clothes for the needy, or give blood. All of these options, and more, are valuable contributions to your community, *in addition to* your responsible financial giving.

The Benefits

When you look at the Biblical concept of the tithe, the understanding that God has entrusted you with certain resources to be managed, and that you will one day be held accountable for your management, you can see it is in your interest to examine your personal finances.

Furthermore, I hope you can see now that BEFORE you examine your budget, get a handle on your debt, and manage to save something for your future, it's important to decide in your heart what is appropriate to give, of your money AND time, towards things that will glorify God.

God's promise is He will bless us for it.....

LIVE SIMPLY… AND GENEROUSLY

*Do not store up for yourselves treasures on earth,
where moth and rust destroy, and where thieves break in and steal.
But store up for yourselves treasures in heaven,
where moth and rust do not destroy,
and where thieves do not break in and steal.
For where your treasure is, there your heart will be also*

–Matthew 6:19-21

The current consumer culture is very persuasive. It woos us with a barrage of messages: we deserve to have everything we desire; when we have everything we want, then we will be complete; we will become the objects of desire, becoming even gods ourselves. We watch, fascinated at the rise, and then in horror at the fall, of stars like Brittany Spears and Miley Cyrus who "prove" it's possible to attain our desires. Watching the choices these celebrities make, we can buy easily into all the illusions, citing them as proof it's not only possible, but also desirable to have this kind of lifestyle.

This culture is a mirage, however, created by people whose only goal is to get wealthy at your expense. They count on your belief in these enticing messages and in your willingness to constantly spend money to pursue these goals. This consumer culture began way back with the advent of credit cards, when we saw DE Beers capitalize on Marilyn Monroe's song "Diamonds are a Girl's Best Friend" to completely turn around the failing diamond market.

Prior to this, diamonds were not the engagement ring of choice. After the price of diamonds collapsed in the Great Depression, in 1938, De Beers planted the impression a man should spend two months salary on an engagement ring. In 1947, De Beers coupled the image of a target cost with their enduring slogan, "Diamonds are Forever". Then, in 1955, two years after "Gentlemen

Prefer Blondes" was screened, DE Beers hit a home run with the greatest advertising campaign on the 20th Century. They featured Marilyn Monroe in their "Diamonds are a Girl's Best Friend" marketing campaign. Through their advertising campaign, they secured the notion as gospel in virtually everyone's minds that not only is a diamond the most enduring substance  for an engagement ring, but also it is the only desirable gem to consider. To this day, many men strive to spend at least 2 month's salary on a ring before popping the question.

The problem with this whole consumer culture is it's a never-ending treadmill. There will always be seductive advertising campaigns and something new to buy. Those wooing you don't care what happens to you at all. They want only your money and don't care if you go bankrupt.

I remember a sermon once that started with an illustration of a church supper at a country church. After elaborately describing the delicious roast beef and mashed potato dinner, the Pastor went on to say if a particular older lady asked you to 'keep your fork' while she cleared the table, you knew there was an amazing dessert - that the best was yet to come.

Jesus' message is different in two ways: He knows the best of life is not here on this earth, but the best is yet to come; and wealth beyond our wildest dreams is available to us, if only we are

© STEVE PUERSTEN, 2014

willing to forego some of the pleasures promised by this consumer culture and invest in our future. He expects us to spend our money in ways that will benefit others, as well as ourselves.

Let's look at what Jesus says about raising the standard for tithing again:

*And he sat down opposite the treasury,
and began observing how the people were putting money
into the treasury; and many rich people were putting in large sums.
A poor widow came and put in two small copper coins.
Calling His disciples to Him, He said to them,
Truly I say to you, this poor widow put in more
than all the contributors to the treasury;
for they all put in out of their surplus, but she, out of her poverty,
put in all she owned, all she had to live on*

–Mark 12:41-44

Paul understood this message very well. After meeting Jesus on the road to Damascus and his conversion, he proceeded to give up a comfortable life of a Pharisee for the uncertainties of the life of a travelling preacher of the word. In the book of Philippians he says;

*I have learned to be content whatever the circumstances.
I know what it is to be in need, and I know what it is to have plenty.
I have learned the secret of being content in any and every situation,
whether well fed or hungry, whether living in plenty or in want.
I can do all this through him who gives me strength*

~ Philippians 4:11-13

© STEVE PUERSTEN, 2014

Now that we have seen both Jesus' expectation for us to give sacrificially, and Paul's teaching regarding being content, what do we do now? How do we reconcile what we have learned with our lives as they stand now?

Life is so full and many demands pull us in every direction. In fact, there are so many demands on our money, which is already so dear. How do we find a way to give sacrificially when, as it is, we have a hard time making our money stretch?

The answer is simple. Or should I say simply.

First of all, make God the centre of every aspect of your life. Since God created you, He knows what is best for you - in all ways. Become familiar with God's expectations in every area of your life, and to put it into practice.

Earlier, I established Jesus raised the bar from the Old Testament legal system so you understand the model of firstfruits still applies. Your next step is to establish what you are going to give and to give it first, before all of the other demands on your income.

Third, establish what you really need in your life and do not accumulate more. Do you need a larger home? Do you need more than one car? Do you need the biggest, best and most elaborate TV out there? Once you come to grips with your needs, as opposed to your desires, you will free up more resources to give back to God.

Finally, giving back to God encompasses more than just giving to the Church, although, certainly, you need to support your local church so your Pastor gets paid and the church has sufficient resources to carry out its mandate to the world.

© STEVE PUERSTEN, 2014

> *The ground of a certain rich man produced a good crop.*
> *He thought to himself, What shall I do? I have no place to store my crops.*
> *Then he said, this is what I'll do. I will tear down my barns*
> *and build bigger ones, and there I will store all my grain and my goods.*
> *And I'll say to myself, You have plenty of good things I*
> *aid up for many years. Take life easy; eat drink and be merry.*
> *But God said to him You fool!*
> *This very night your life will be demanded of you.*
> *Then who will get what you have prepared for yourself*
>
> –Luke 12:16-20

Notice the rich man talks about using his wealth only for his own comfort. Yet, while it is important to plan, save and handle our financial resources responsibly, the Bible makes it clear we are to be generous in our community as well.

Just like the rich man, none of us knows when God will demand our lives from us. When He does, will you be able to take any of it with you? At the very best, what you have accumulated will be passed on to your children. At worst, it may left in the hands of a trustee to do with as they see fit.

If you take the time to contribute to those around you - to your church, your neighbours and causes close to your heart - not only do you improve your community, but also you create an opportunity to be remembered fondly, to create a legacy of generosity which can serve as an inspiration to those who follow behind you.

© STEVE PUERSTEN, 2014

'No servant can serve two masters:
for either he will hate the one, and love the other;
or else he will hold to the one, and despise the other.
You cannot serve God and money
-Luke 16:13

Ultimately, it comes down to a choice. If Jesus' message you cannot serve both God and money is true, then what can you do? Many go to their graves worshiping money, pursuing it and the things it can buy, and get nothing but temporary pleasure from it.

On the other hand, Jesus promises more. He says: If you live a little less and give a little more, the gain is far greater than we can ever imagine.

SO WHO WILL YOU SERVE?

MEET THE AUTHOR

About Steve Puersten

Steve provides bookkeeping services for both private enterprise and non-profit organizations, primarily local Churches. He enjoys teaching clients and colleagues alike how to create simple systems to manage their financial lives. His interest in teaching others is part of a greater focus - helping create and nurture a symbiotic small business community, in which enterprises work together for a greater goal. In fact, Steve is so passionate about this concept, he has volunteered locally to foster the combined health of small business and local communities for over 10 years. Steve plays guitar, writes his own music and lives in the Toronto Area with his two talented daughters.

Stay in Touch with Steve

Steve would love it receive your questions and comments via email or the following social media platforms:

Email: Go to: http://puerstenbookkeeping.com/ContactUs/
Linkedin: **https://www.linkedin.com/in/stevepuersten**
Facebook: FB.com/ Puersten-Bookkeeping/172557966169915
Twitter: twitter.com/StevePuersten

www.ingramcontent.com/pod-product-compliance
Lightning Source LLC
Chambersburg PA
CBHW040918180526
45159CB00002BA/514